# ESTATE PUBLICATIONS

# WINCHESTER
## NEW ALRESFORD · SUTTON SCOTNEY ·

C000197257

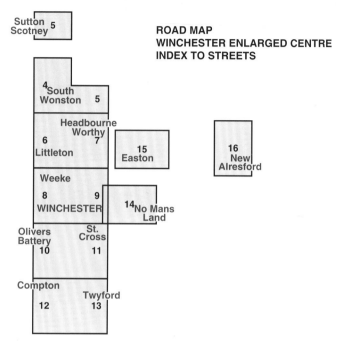

| | |
|---|---|
| ROAD MAP | Page 2 |
| WINCHESTER ENLARGED CENTRE | Page 3 |
| INDEX TO STREETS | Page 17 |

Sutton Scotney 5

4 South Wonston 5

Headbourne Worthy

6 7
Littleton

15 Easton

16 New Alresford

Weeke

8 9
WINCHESTER

14 No Mans Land

Olivers Battery 10

St. Cross 11

Compton 12

Twyford 13

---

## Scale of street plans: 4 Inches to 1 Mile (unless otherwise stated)

| | |
|---|---|
| Motorway | |
| 'A' Road / Dual | |
| 'B' Road / Dual | |
| Minor Road / Dual | |
| Track | |
| Pedestrianized | |
| Railway / Station | |
| Footpath | |

Every effort has been made to verify the accuracy of information in this book but the publishers cannot accept responsibility for expense or loss caused by an error or omission. Information that will be of assistance to the user of the maps will be welcomed.

The representation on these maps of a road, track or path is no evidence of the existence of a right of way.

| | |
|---|---|
| ~ | Stream / River |
| Lock ~ | Canal |
| → | One-way Street |
| P | Car Park |
| C | Public Convenience |
| i | Tourist Information |
| + | Place of Worship |
| ● | Post Office |

Street plans prepared and published by ESTATE PUBLICATIONS, Bridewell House, TENTERDEN, KENT. The Publishers acknowledge the co-operation of the local authorities of towns represented in this atlas.

Ordnance Survey® This product includes mapping data licensed from Ordnance Survey® with the permission of the Controller of Her Majesty's Stationery Office.

ISBN 1 84192 217 X

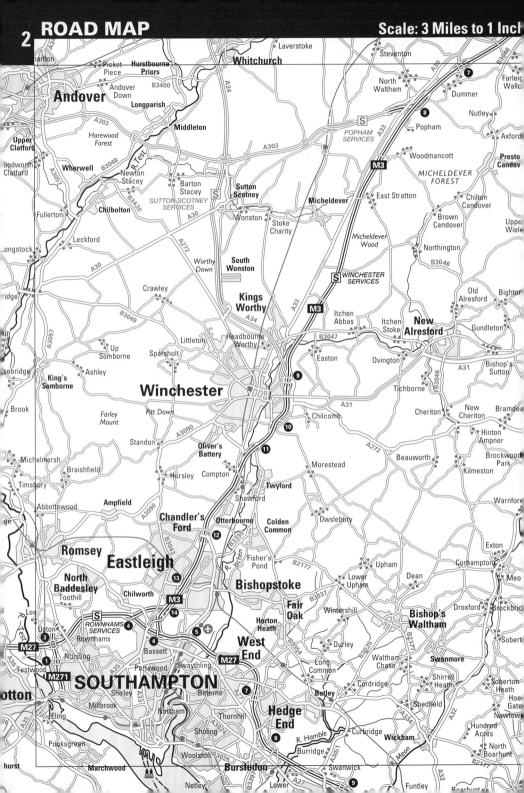

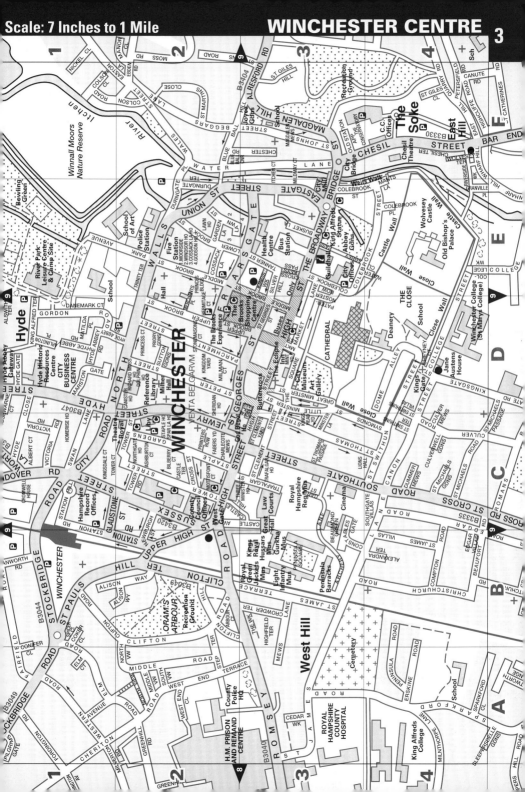

**4**

A     B     C     D

A34

WONSTON LANE

1

Tumulus ☼

2

☼ Tumulus

LANE

South Wonston Farm

Sanctuary Farm

ALRESFORD DRO

WEST HILL ROAD NORTH

Larkwhistle Farm

STAINERS LA

**South Wonston**

GOLDFINCH WY

3

CHAUCER WAY

SPRUCE CL

LONGBARROW CL

WAVERLEY

ROWAN

MARKSON RD

STAVEDOWN RD

WRIGHTS

WRIGHTS

KEATS CL

BURNS CL

CLOSE

NORRIS CL ●

BROOKE WY

HOME

HALL

ROAD

PINE DR

PLANE CL

DOWNS

ORCHARD RD

GROVES WY

NURSERY CL

HOLLY WY

RD RD

DOWNLANDS

WALNUT TREE CL

SANDYS WY

DOWN CHERRY CL

BORMAN CL

LOVELL WY

ANDERS RD

ARMSTRONG

WEST HILL RD STH

WAVERLEY GREEN

CHRISTMAS

South Wonston Primary School

ROAD

LOWER

4

Water Tower ○

LOWER ROAD

ROAD

Race Course Cottages

Field System

Worthy Grove

Water Tower ○

BLACKWELL

BLACKWELL

COOPERS CL

Worthy Down Camp

5

**Worthy Down**

REES RD

RD

MALPASS ●

ROLL

COATE

BYRNE CL

DRIVE

STANHAM CL

COWLEY DR

ROAD

CONNAUGHT

HILL

CHRIS

6

A272

A34

Gallops

A     B     ▼6     C     D

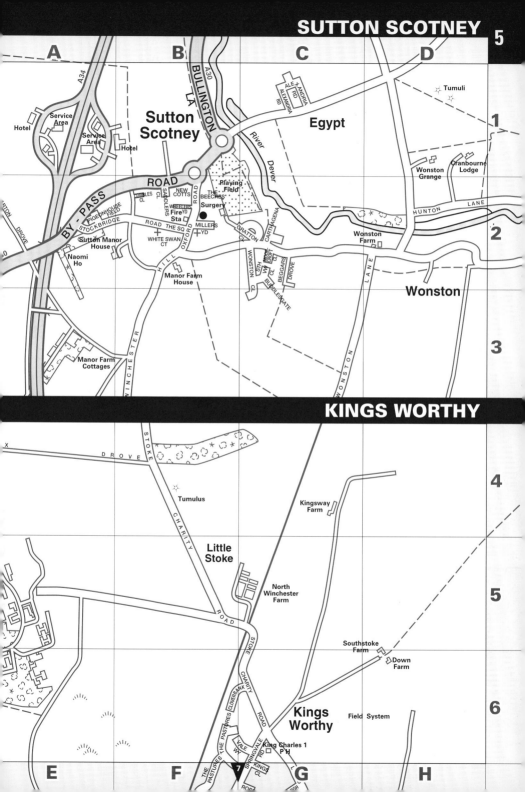

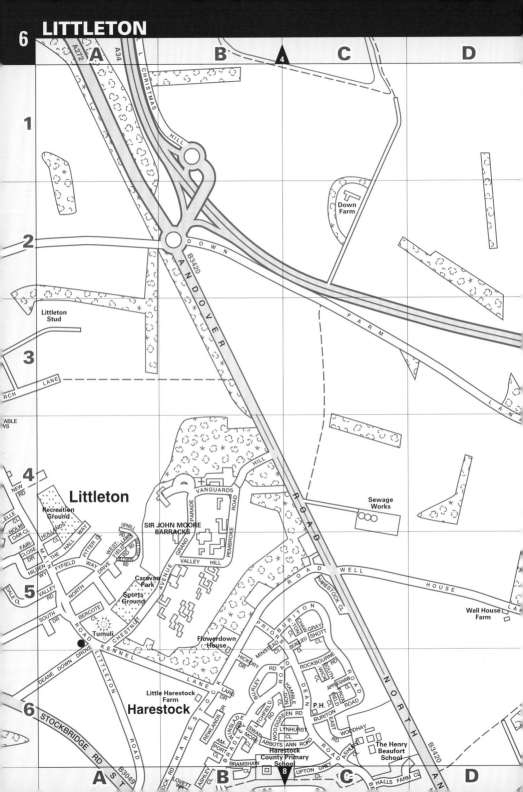

LITTLETON

Littleton

Harestock

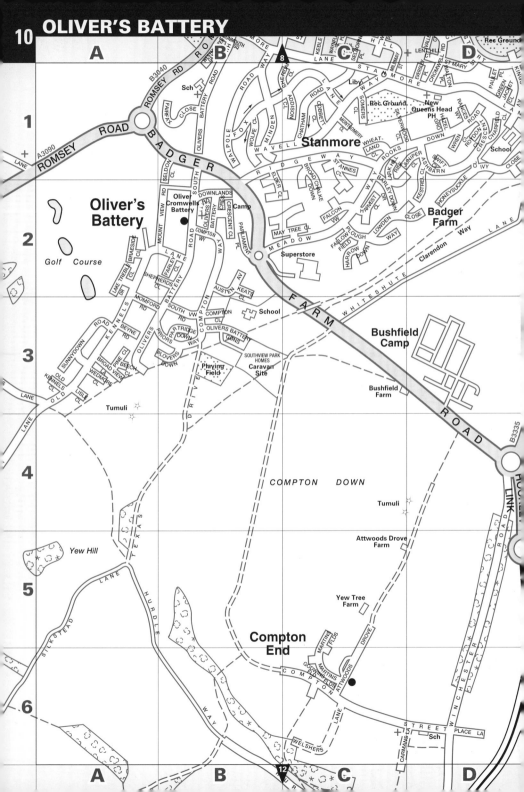

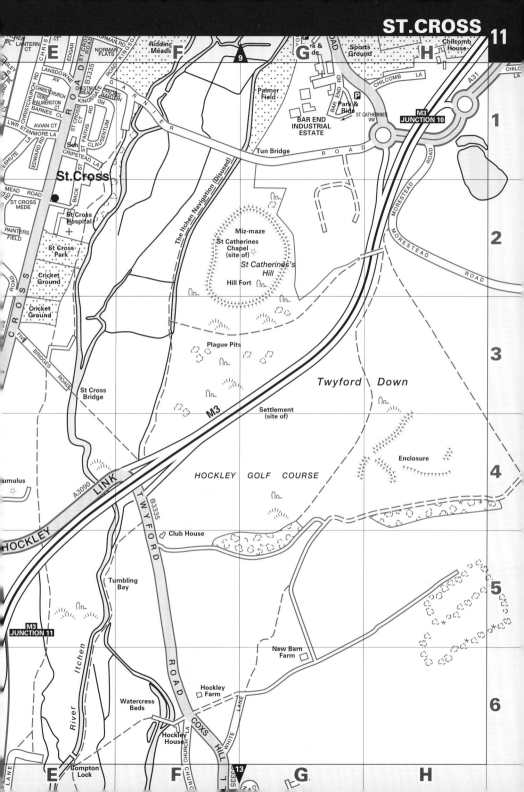

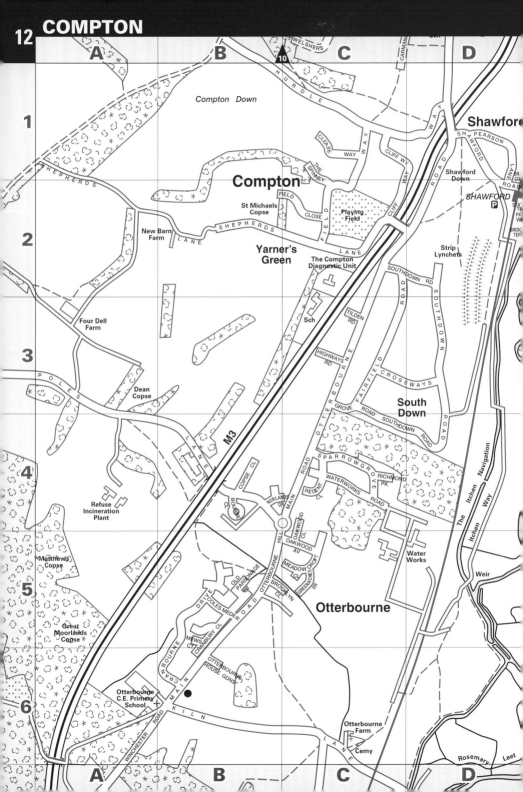

**A**  **B**  **C**  **D**

WELSHERS

Compton Down

Shawfor

Compton

St Michaels
Copse

New Barn
Farm

Yarner's
Green

SHEPHERDS

LANE

The Compton
Diagnostic Unit

Playing
Field

FIELD CLOSE

THE SPINNEY

CLEASE WAY

WAY

CLIFF WY

CLIFF

LANE

HURDLE

WAY

Shawford
Down

SHAWFORD

ROAD

PEARSON

SHAWFORD

ROAD

Strip
Lynchets

Four Dell
Farm

Sch

Dean
Copse

POLES

LANE

HIGHWAYS
RD

TILDEN
RD

SOUTHDOWN RD

ROAD

SOUTHDOWN

CROSSWAYS

South
Down

OTTERBOURNE

GROVE

FAIRFIELD

SOUTHDOWN ROAD

ROAD

M3

COPSE CL

BOURNE

NORLANDS
DR

HILL

MAIN

REGENT

OAKWOOD

SPARROW GROVE

WATERWORKS

RICHMOND
PK

ROAD

Refuse
Incineration
Plant

Matthews
Copse

MEADOW
CL

OAKWOOD
AV

BROOKLYN
CL

GREENACRES CROFT DR

Water
Works

The Itchen Navigation

Itchen Way

Weir

Great
Moorlands
Copse

OLD
PARSONAGE
RD

OTTERBOURNE ROAD

Otterbourne

DRIVE

COLES MEDE

MEWSBURY
CT

CRANBURY CL

OTTERBOURNE
HOUSE GDNS

MAIN

ROAD

WINCHESTER ROAD

KILN

LANE

Otterbourne
C.E. Primary
School

Otterbourne
Farm

Cemy

Rosemary

Leet

**A**  **B**  **C**  **D**

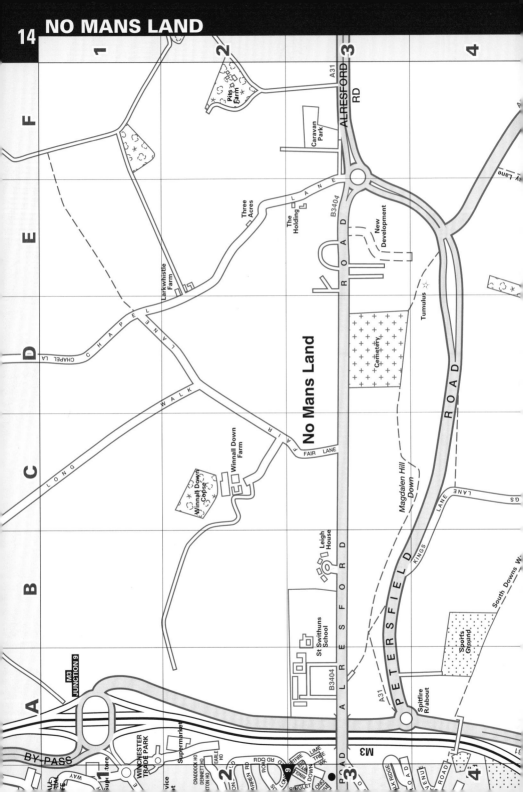

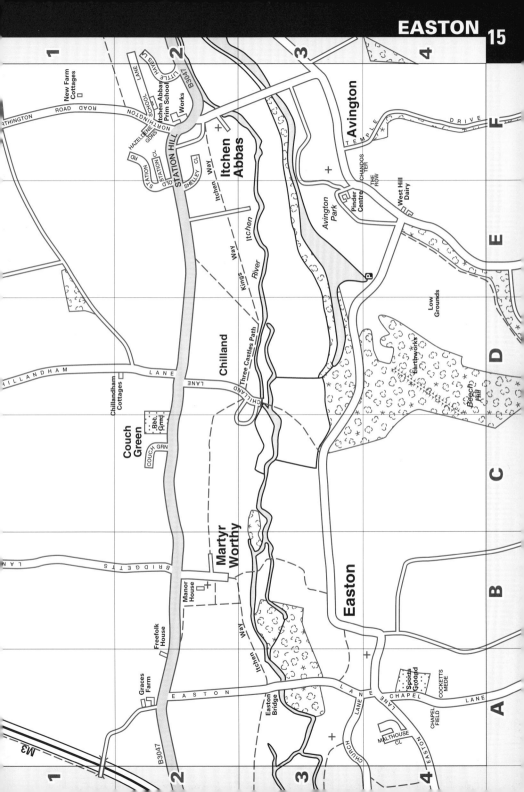

New Farm Cottages

ORTHINGTON ROAD ROAD

Itchen Abbas Prim School
Works

B3047

HAZELDENE SCHOOL LANE
LITTLE HAYES LANE
NORTHINGTON RD
STATION GDNS
OLD STATION CL
STATION HILL
SHELLEY CL

Itchen Abbas

Avington

TEMPLE
CHANDOS TER
THE ROW
DRIVE

West Hill Dairy

Itchen Way

Avington Park

Pinder Centre

River Itchen

King's Way

Chilland

Three Castles Path

CHILLAND LANE

Low Grounds

Earthworks

Beech Hill

CHILLANDHAM LANE

Chillandham Cottages

COUCH GRN

PH

Couch Green

Rec. Grnd

Easton

Martyr Worthy

BRIDGETS LANE

Manor House

Freefolk House

Itchen Way

Graces Farm

EASTON LANE

B3047

M3

Easton Bridge

Sports Ground

COCKETTS MEDE

CHAPEL FIELD

CHAPEL LANE

CHURCH LANE

EASTON LANE

MALTHOUSE CL

LANE

F
E
D
C
B
A

1
2
3
4

**A** **B** **C** **D**

Old Alresford

New Alresford

The Soke

e Index includes some
mes for which there is
ufficient space on the
aps. These names are
dicated by an * and are
lowed by the nearest
joining thoroughfare.

| | | | | | | | | |
|---|---|---|---|---|---|---|---|
| bey Hill Cl SO23 | 9 E2 | Bedfield La SO23 | 7 F5 | Castle Ter SO23 | 3 C2 | Compton Cl SO22 | 10 B3 | Dyson Dr SO23 | 9 F1 |
| bey Hill Rd SO23 | 9 E2 | Beech Cl SO22 | 10 A3 | Cathedral Vw SO23 | 9 F6 | Compton Rd SO23 | 3 B4 | | |
| bey Pass SO23 | 3 E3 | Beech Copse SO22 | 8 A3 | Cavendish Gro SO23 | 9 F1 | Compton St SO11 | 10 C6 | Earle Ho SO23 | 9 H3 |
| bots Ann Rd SO23 | 6 B6 | Beech Rd SO24 | 16 D4 | Cedar Cl SO23 | 7 F1 | Compton Way SO22 | 10 B2 | East Hill SO23 | 3 F4 |
| bots Worthy Rd | | Beggars Dro SO21 | 5 C2 | Cedar Ct SO23 | 8 D6 | Coney Grn SO23 | 9 E2 | East St SO24 | 16 D4 |
| O21 | 7 H4 | Beggars La SO23 | 3 F2 | Cedar Walk SO22 | 3 A3 | Conifer Cl SO22 | 3 A1 | East Woodhay Rd | |
| botts Cl SO23 | 9 F2 | Bell Ho SO24 | 16 D6 | Cedarwood SO23 | 7 H2 | Coniston Gro SO24 | 16 D6 | SO22 | 6 C6 |
| botts Ct SO23 | 9 E2 | Beneden Grn SO24 | 16 C6 | Chalk Ridge SO23 | 9 H5 | Connaught Rd SO21 | 4 A5 | Eastacre SO22 | 8 D2 |
| botts Rd SO23 | 9 E1 | Bentley Cl SO23 | 7 F3 | Chandos Ter SO23 | 15 F4 | Constables Gate SO23 | 3 B3 | Eastgate St SO23 | 3 E3 |
| orn Cl SO23 | 8 B2 | Bercote Cl SO22 | 6 A5 | Chapel Fld SO21 | 15 A4 | Coopers Cl SO23 | 4 B5 | Easton La, | |
| ddison Cl SO22 | 10 C1 | Bere Cl SO22 | 8 C2 | Chapel La, | | Coppice Cl SO22 | 8 B3 | Easton SO21 | 15 A2 |
| lie Cnr SO22 | 8 D6 | Bereweeke Av SO22 | 8 C1 | Easton SO21 | 15 A4 | Copse Cl SO21 | 12 B4 | Easton La, | |
| lie Rd SO22 | 8 D6 | Bereweeke Cl SO22 | 8 C2 | Chapel La, | | Coram Cl SO23 | 9 F2 | Winchester SO23 | 3 F2 |
| ert Ct SO23 | 3 C1 | Bereweeke Rd SO22 | 8 C3 | No Mans Land SO21 | 14 D1 | Corfe Ct SO24 | 16 C6 | Easton La Bsns Pk | |
| ders Ct SO24 | 16 D4 | Bereweeke Way SO22 | 8 D2 | Charfield Cl SO22 | 10 D1 | Cossack La SO23 | 3 E2 | SO23 | 9 G4 |
| exandra Ter SO23 | 3 B4 | Berry La SO21 | 13 F1 | Charlecote Mws SO23 | 3 C2 | Cossack Lane Ho SO23 | 3 E2 | Ebden Rd SO23 | 3 F2 |
| exandria Rd SO21 | 5 C1 | Beyne Rd SO22 | 10 A3 | Charles Cl SO23 | 9 F2 | Couch Grn SO21 | 15 C2 | Edgar Rd SO23 | 3 B4 |
| son Way SO22 | 3 B1 | Bilberry Ct SO23 | 3 C2 | Chatham Rd SO22 | 10 C1 | Court Rd SO23 | 7 G4 | Edgar Villas SO23 | 8 D5 |
| esford Dro SO21 | 4 D3 | Birinus Rd SO23 | 9 F3 | Chaucer Cl SO21 | 4 C3 | Courtenay Rd SO23 | 9 E2 | Edinburgh Rd SO23 | 7 G1 |
| esford Rd SO21,23 | 3 F3 | Blackthorn Cl SO21 | 4 B4 | Chaucer Ind Est | | Covey Way SO24 | 16 B5 | Edington Rd SO23 | 9 E2 |
| switha Ter SO23 | 3 D1 | Blackwell Rd SO23 | 4 A5 | SO23 | 9 G3 | Cowley Dr SO21 | 4 C6 | Edward Rd SO23 | 11 E1 |
| nport Ct SO22 | 6 B6 | Blue Ball Cnr SO23 | 3 F2 | Chaundler Rd SO23 | 9 F2 | Coxs Hill SO21 | 11 F6 | Edward Ter SO24 | 16 D4 |
| ders Rd SO21 | 4 C4 | Blue Ball Hill SO23 | 3 F2 | Chawton Cl SO22 | 6 C5 | Craddock Ho SO23 | 9 H3 | Egbert Rd SO23 | 9 E3 |
| dover Rd SO23 | 3 C1 | Borman Way SO21 | 4 C3 | Cheriton Cl SO22 | 8 C3 | Cranbourne Dr SO21 | 12 B6 | Elder Cl SO22 | 10 B1 |
| dover Rd North | | Boscobel Rd SO22 | 8 D3 | Cheriton Rd SO22 | 3 A1 | Cranbury Cl SO21 | 12 B6 | Eling Cl SO23 | 8 C1 |
| O22 | 6 B2 | Bourne Cl SO21 | 12 B4 | Cherry Cl SO21 | 4 C4 | Cranworth Rd SO22 | 3 B1 | Elizabeth Cl SO23 | 7 G1 |
| dover Rd Retail Pk | | Bourne La SO21 | 13 F1 | Chesil St SO23 | 3 F3 | Crescent Cl SO22 | 10 B2 | Ellingham Cl SO24 | 16 C4 |
| O23 | 9 E3 | Bournefields SO21 | 13 G1 | Chesil Ter SO23 | 3 F4 | Cripstead La SO23 | 11 E1 | Elm Ct SO22 | 3 A1 |
| pledown Cl SO24 | 16 D6 | Boyne Mead Rd SO23 | 7 G3 | Chester Rd SO23 | 3 F3 | Crockford Ho SO24 | 16 D4 | Elm Rd, | |
| pleshaw Cl SO22 | 6 C6 | Boyne Rise SO23 | 7 G2 | Chestnut Av SO22 | 6 A5 | Cromwell Ho SO23 | 3 C1 | Alresford SO24 | 16 C5 |
| pour Ct SO22 | 3 B2 | Bradley Peak SO22 | 8 B2 | Chestnut Mead SO23 | 11 E1 | Cromwell Rd SO22 | 10 D1 | Elm Rd, | |
| chery La SO23 | 3 B3 | Bradley Rd SO22 | 6 B6 | Chestnut Walk SO24 | 16 D5 | Cross Keys Pass SO23 | 3 E3 | Winchester SO22 | 3 A1 |
| e Cl SO24 | 16 C3 | Braeside Cl SO22 | 6 B6 | Cheyney Ct SO23 | 3 D4 | Cross St SO23 | 3 C2 | Ennerdale Gdns SO24 | 16 D5 |
| e Gdns SO24 | 16 C3 | Bramble Hill SO24 | 16 C5 | Chilbolton Av SO22 | 8 B4 | Crossways SO21 | 12 C3 | Erasmus Pk SO23 | 9 G3 |
| ington Pl SO23 | 3 D1 | Bramshaw Cl SO22 | 6 B6 | Chilbolton Ct SO22 | 8 B5 | Crouchers Cft SO22 | 8 A2 | Erskine Rd SO22 | 3 A4 |
| mstrong Cl SO21 | 4 C4 | Brandy Mt SO24 | 16 D4 | Chilcomb La SO23 | 11 H1 | Crowder Ter SO23 | 3 B3 | Evelyn Mws SO24 | 16 C4 |
| hur Rd SO23 | 9 E3 | Branksome Cl SO22 | 8 A6 | Chilland La SO21 | 15 D3 | Culley Vw SO24 | 16 C5 | Eversley Pl SO22 | 10 D1 |
| undel Cl SO24 | 16 C6 | Brassey Rd SO22 | 9 E3 | Chillandham La SO21 | 15 D1 | Culver Mws SO23 | 3 C4 | | |
| hley Cl SO22 | 8 B1 | Braxton Ho SO23 | 9 H3 | Chiltern Ct SO24 | 16 D5 | Culver Rd SO23 | 3 C4 | Fabers Yd SO23 | 3 C2 |
| hmore Rd SO22 | 8 B3 | Brendon SO23 | 9 E2 | Christchurch Gdns | | Culverwell Gdns SO23 | 3 C4 | Fair La SO21 | 14 C3 |
| woods Dro SO21 | 10 C6 | Brewers La SO23 | 13 F3 | SO23 | 11 E1 | Cundell Way SO23 | 7 F1 | Fair Vw SO24 | 16 C6 |
| sten Av SO22 | 10 B2 | Brewhouse Yd SO24 | 16 D4 | Christchurch Rd SO23 | 3 B4 | | | Fairdown Cl SO23 | 9 G5 |
| sten Cl SO23 | 9 F2 | Bridge Cotts SO21 | 12 D1 | Christmas Hill SO21 | 4 A3 | Danemark Ct SO23 | 3 D1 | Fairfax Cl SO22 | 10 B1 |
| enue Rd SO22 | 3 A1 | Bridge Rd SO24 | 16 B4 | Church La, | | Danes Rd SO23 | 9 E3 | Fairfield Rd, | |
| ian Ct SO23 | 11 E1 | Bridge St SO23 | 3 E3 | Kings Worthy SO23 | 7 G4 | Dawn Gdns SO22 | 8 B6 | Shawford SO21 | 12 C3 |
| | | Bridge Ter SO23 | 12 D2 | Church La, | | Dean Cl SO22 | 8 B2 | Fairfield Rd, | |
| ck St SO23 | 11 E2 | Bridgetts La SO21 | 15 B2 | Twyford SO21 | 13 F1 | Dean La SO22 | 8 A2 | Winchester SO22 | 3 A1 |
| dger Farm Rd SO22 | 10 A1 | Broad Chalke Down | | Church La, | | Deane Down Dro SO22 | 6 A6 | Falcon Vw SO22 | 10 C2 |
| gent Cl SO23 | 9 G4 | SO22 | 10 C1 | Winchester SO21 | 15 A3 | Dell Rd SO23 | 9 E2 | Fallow Fld SO22 | 10 C2 |
| ley Cl SO22 | 8 C6 | Broad St SO24 | 16 D3 | Churchfields SO21 | 13 F2 | De-Lucy Av SO24 | 16 B5 | Farley Cl SO23 | 10 B2 |
| r End Ind Est | | Broad View SO22 | 10 A3 | Churchill Cl SO23 | 7 G1 | Denham Cl SO23 | 9 E2 | Felmer Dr SO23 | 7 G3 |
| O23 | 11 G1 | Brooke Cl SO23 | 7 G1 | City Bsns Centre | | Dennett Ho SO23 | 9 H3 | Field Cl SO21 | 12 B2 |
| r End Rd SO23 | 9 F6 | Brooklyn Cl SO23 | 12 B5 | SO23 | 3 D1 | Derwent Gdns SO24 | 16 D6 | Field End SO23 | 7 G3 |
| rfield Cl SO23 | 9 F6 | Browning Dr SO22 | 8 C4 | City Rd SO23 | 3 C1 | Devenish Rd SO22 | 8 C1 | Field Way SO21 | 12 C2 |
| ring Rd SO23 | 9 G5 | Buddlesgate SO21 | 5 C2 | Clausentum Rd SO23 | 11 E1 | Dickenson Walk SO24 | 16 C6 | Finches La SO23 | 13 F2 |
| ley Down Dr SO22 | 10 C1 | Bullington La SO21 | 5 B1 | Clease Way SO21 | 12 C1 | Dolphin Hill SO21 | 13 F2 | Fiona Cl SO23 | 9 G4 |
| rnes Cl SO23 | 11 E1 | Buriton Rd SO22 | 6 B5 | Cliff Way SO21 | 12 C2 | Dolphin Ho SO23 | 3 D2 | Firmstone Rd SO23 | 9 G4 |
| rtholomew Cl SO23 | 9 E3 | Burley Rd SO22 | 6 B6 | Clifton Hill SO22 | 3 B2 | Dome Alley SO23 | 3 D4 | Firs Cres SO23 | 7 F1 |
| rton Dro SO21 | 5 A2 | Burne Cl SO21 | 4 B5 | Clifton Rd SO22 | 3 B2 | Domum Rd SO23 | 9 F6 | Five Bridges Rd SO23 | 11 E3 |
| singstoke Rd SO23 | 7 H4 | Burnett Cl SO22 | 8 B1 | Clifton Ter SO22 | 3 B2 | Donnington Ct SO23 | 9 F2 | Fivefields Cl SO23 | 9 G6 |
| ttery Hill SO22 | 8 A6 | Burns Cl SO21 | 4 C3 | Cloverbank SO23 | 5 F6 | Dorian Gro SO23 | 16 B5 | Fivefields Rd SO23 | 9 G5 |
| aufort Rd SO23 | 3 B4 | Busket La SO23 | 3 E3 | Coate Dr SO21 | 4 B5 | Dover Cl SO24 | 16 C6 | Fleming Rd SO22 | 8 B1 |
| aulieu Cl SO22 | 6 C5 | Buttermere Gdns | | Cobbett Cl SO22 | 10 C1 | Down Farm La SO22 | 6 B2 | Forbes Rd SO23 | 7 G2 |
| aumont Grn SO23 | 3 B3 | SO24 | 16 D5 | Cobbles SO21 | 5 B2 | Down Gate SO24 | 16 C6 | Fordington Av SO22 | 8 C4 |
| | | By-Pass Rd SO23 | 5 A2 | Cocketts Mede SO21 | 15 A4 | Downlands Rd SO22 | 10 B2 | Fordington Rd SO22 | 3 A1 |
| | | Byron Av SO22 | 8 B4 | Coker Cl SO22 | 3 B1 | Downlands Way, | | Fox La SO22 | 10 B1 |
| | | | | Colbourne Ct SO23 | 9 F2 | Winchester SO21 | 4 C4 | Frampton Way SO23 | 7 G3 |
| | | Campion Way SO23 | 7 G3 | Colden La SO24 | 16 D2 | Downlands Way, | | Francis Gdns SO23 | 9 F1 |
| | | Canister Ho SO23 | 3 D2 | Colebrook Pl SO23 | 3 E4 | Winchester SO21 | 4 B4 | Franklin Rd SO21 | 13 F1 |
| | | Canon St SO23 | 3 C4 | Colebrook St SO23 | 3 E3 | Downs Rd SO21 | 4 A3 | Fraser Rd SO23 | 7 G1 |
| | | Canute Rd SO23 | 3 F4 | Coles Cl SO21 | 13 G1 | Downside Rd SO22 | 8 A2 | Friarsgate SO23 | 3 D2 |
| | | Carisbrooke Cl SO24 | 16 C6 | Coles Mede SO21 | 12 B5 | Drayton Cl SO22 | 8 B6 | Fromond Rd SO22 | 8 B1 |
| | | Carmans La SO21 | 10 C6 | College Ct SO23 | 9 F6 | Drove Cl SO21 | 13 E3 | Froxfield Cl SO23 | 6 C6 |
| | | Carpenters SO24 | 16 C5 | College St SO23 | 3 D4 | Drove La SO24 | 16 C5 | Fulflood Cl SO23 | 8 C4 |
| | | Carthagena SO21 | 5 C2 | College Walk SO23 | 3 E4 | Drummond Cl SO22 | 11 E1 | Furley Cl SO23 | 9 G4 |
| | | Castle Av SO23 | 3 C3 | Colley Cl SO23 | 9 F1 | Dummer Mws SO23 | 3 C4 | Fyfield Way SO22 | 6 A5 |
| | | Castle Hill SO23 | 3 C3 | Colson Cl SO23 | 3 E2 | Durngate Pl SO23 | 3 E2 | | |
| | | Castle Rise SO23 | 7 G1 | Colson Rd SO23 | 3 F2 | Durngate Ter SO23 | 3 E2 | Gar St SO23 | 3 C3 |

Garbett Rd SO23 9 G4
Garden La SO23 3 E2
Garnier Rd SO23 11 E1
Gatekeeper Cl SO23 9 G4
General Johnson Ct SO22 8 B6
George Eyston Dr SO22 8 C6
Gillingham Cl SO23 7 G3
Gladstone St SO23 3 B1
Godson Ho SO23 3 E3
Godwin Cl SO22 8 B1
Godwins Fld SO21 10 C6
Goldfinch Way SO23 4 D3
Gordon Av SO23 9 G6
Gordon Rd SO23 3 D1
Goring Fld SO22 8 B3
Grafton SO23 8 D6
Grand Par SO22 6 B5
Grange Cl, Alresford SO24 16 B5
Grange Cl, Winchester SO23 11 E2
Grange Rd, Alresford SO24 16 B5
Grange Rd, Winchester SO23 11 E3
Granville Pl SO23 3 E4
Gratton Cl SO21 5 B2
Grayshott Cl SO22 6 C5
Great Field Rd SO22 8 C1
Great Minster St SO23 3 D3
Green Cl, Alresford SO24 16 D1
Green Cl, Headbourne Worthy SO23 7 E5
Green Cl, South Wonston SO21 4 D4
Green Jacket Cl SO22 10 D1
Green La SO22 8 C3
Green Park Cl SO23 9 F1
Greenacres Dr SO21 12 C5
Greenhill Av SO22 8 D4
Greenhill Cl SO22 8 C4
Greenhill Rd SO22 3 A2
Greenhill Ter SO22 8 C4
Grosvenor Dr SO23 9 F1
Grove Rd SO21 12 C3
Grovelands Rd SO22 8 A3
Groves Cl SO21 4 B4

Haig Rd SO24 16 D4
Halls Farm Cl SO22 8 C1
Hambledon Cl SO23 6 C6
Hampton La SO22 8 B3
Hanover Lodge SO23 9 F6
Hare La SO21 13 F4
Harestock Cl SO22 6 C5
Harestock Rd SO22 8 A1
Harrow Down SO22 10 C2
Harvest Cl SO22 10 C2
Harwood Pl SO23 7 G2
Hasted Dr SO24 16 C6
Hatherley Rd SO22 8 D3
Hawthorn Cl SO24 16 C5
Haydn Cl SO23 7 G2
Hazel Gro SO22 10 D1
Hazeldene Gdns SO21 15 F2
Hazeley Rd SO21 13 F2
Headley Cl SO24 16 D6
Hermitage Ct SO23 3 D2
Hickory Dr SO22 6 B6
High St, Twyford SO21 13 F4
High St, Winchester SO23 3 C2
High Trees Dr SO22 8 C2
Highbridge Rd SO21 13 E6
Highcliffe Rd SO23 3 F4
Highfield SO21 13 F3
Highfield Av SO21 13 F3
Highfield Ter SO22 3 B3
Highmount Cl SO23 9 G5

Highways Rd SO21 12 C3
Hill Rise SO21 13 F3
Hillside Cl SO23 8 B2
Hillside Rd, Littleton SO22 6 A5
Hillside Rd, Winchester SO22 8 A3
Hilltop SO22 6 A5
Hinton Flds SO23 7 G4
Hockley Link SO21 10 D4
Holdaway Cl SO23 7 G3
Hollands Cl SO22 6 A5
Homerise Ho SO23 3 C1
Honeysuckle Cl SO22 10 D2
Hookpit Farm La SO23 7 F2
Hornbeam Cl SO21 4 D3
Hubert Rd SO23 11 E2
Hunt Cl SO21 4 D4
Hunton La SO21 5 D2
Hunts La SO21 13 E1
Hurdle Way SO21 12 B1
Hussey Cl SO23 9 F1
Hyde Abbey Rd SO23 3 D1
Hyde Church La SO23 9 E3
Hyde Cl SO23 3 C1
Hyde Gate SO23 3 D1
Hyde House Gdns SO23 9 E3
Hyde St SO23 3 D1

Ilex Cl SO23 7 F2
Imber Rd SO23 9 G4
Itchen Cl SO23 3 E3
Itchen Way SO24 16 A6
Ivy Cl SO22 10 D1

Jacklyns Cl SO24 16 C5
Jacklyns La SO24 16 C5
Jesty Rd SO24 16 B5
Jewry St SO23 3 C2
Juniper Cl SO21 10 C1

Keats Cl, South Wonston SO21 4 C3
Keats Cl, Winchester SO22 10 B2
Keble St SO22 8 B6
Kennel La SO22 6 A5
Kerryfield SO22 8 B5
Kerryfield Mws SO22 8 C5
Kestrel Cl SO22 10 D2
Kilham La SO22 8 A6
Kiln La, Alresford SO24 16 D1
Kiln La, Winchester SO21 12 B6
King Alfred Pl SO23 3 D1
King Alfred Ter SO23 3 D1
King Harold Ct SO23 8 D6
Kingdom Yd SO23 3 D2
Kings Av SO22 10 D1
Kings Cl, Twyford SO21 13 G1
Kings Cl, Winchester SO23 7 G1
Kings Head Yd SO23 3 C3
Kings La SO21 14 B4
Kings Rd SO22 8 A6
Kings Walk SO23 3 E3
Kings Worthy Ct SO23 7 G4
Kings Worthy Link SO23 7 E3
Kingsdale Ct SO23 3 C1
Kingsgate Rd SO23 11 E1
Kingsgate St SO23 3 D4
Kingsley Bungalows SO24 16 B6
Kingsley Pl SO23 8 D6
Knight Cl SO23 9 E2
Kynegils Rd SO22 8 C2

Ladywell La SO24 16 D3
Lainston Cl SO23 8 B2

Lake Dr SO22 10 A2
Langton Cl SO22 8 C3
Langtons Ct SO24 16 D5
Lanham La SO22 8 A2
Lankhills Rd SO23 9 E2
Lansdowne Av SO23 11 E1
Lantern Ct SO23 8 D6
Larch Cl SO23 7 F1
Larg Dr SO22 6 B6
Lark Hill Rise SO22 10 C1
Lawn Ho SO23 3 E2
Lawn Rd SO22 6 A5
Lawn St SO23 3 E2
Lawrence Way SO22 9 F2
Legion La SO23 7 G2
Leicester Way SO23 9 H3
Lent Hill Ct SO22 8 C6
Lime Rd SO24 16 D5
Limetree Walk SO23 9 H4
Lindley Gdns SO24 16 C6
Links Rd SO22 8 C3
Linnets Rd SO24 16 C6
Lions Hall SO23 3 C3
Lisle Cl SO22 10 A3
Lisle Ct SO22 8 D6
Litchfield Rd SO22 6 B6
Little Hayes La SO21 15 F2
Little Minster St SO23 3 D3
Littleton Rd SO22 6 A6
Loader Cl SO23 7 H3
London Rd SO23 7 G5
Long Walk SO21 14 C1
Longbarrow Cl SO21 4 D3
Longfield Rd SO23 9 H4
Longhouse Grn SO23 9 H4
Love La, Twyford SO21 13 G3
Love La, Winchester SO22 8 C3
Lovedon La SO23 7 G1
Lovell Cl SO21 4 C4
Lovells Walk SO24 16 C5
Lovett Walk SO22 8 B1
Lowden Cl SO22 10 C2
Lower Brook St SO23 3 E2
Lower Rd SO21 4 A4
Lower Stanmore La SO23 11 E1
Lynch Cl SO22 8 C2
Lynford Av SO22 8 D2
Lynford Way SO22 8 D2
Lynhurst Cl SO22 6 B6
Lynn Way SO23 7 G3

Magdalen Hill SO23 3 F3
Main Rd, Littleton SO22 6 A5
Main Rd, Otterbourne SO21 12 B6
Main Rd, Twyford SO21 13 F6
Mallard Cl SO24 16 C4
Malmesbury Gdns SO22 8 B2
Malpass Rd SO21 4 B5
Malthouse Cl SO21 15 A4
Maningford Cl SO23 9 F1
Manor Cl SO23 9 G4
Manor Farm Grn SO21 13 F3
Manor Rd SO21 13 F3
Mants La SO21 3 E4
Maple Cl SO24 16 C6
Maple Dr SO21 7 F1
Market La SO23 3 D3
Market St SO23 3 D3
Markson Rd SO21 4 A3
Marston Gate SO23 3 D1
Martins Flds SO21 10 C6
Matilda Pl SO23 3 D1
May Tree Cl SO22 10 B2
Mead Cl SO21 11 E2
Meadow Cl SO24 16 D5

Meadow Way SO22 10 B2
Meadowcroft Cl SO21 12 C5
Meadowland SO23 7 G3
Melrose Ct SO23 8 D6
Merchants Pl SO23 3 D2
Meryon Rd SO24 16 B6
Mews Ct SO21 12 B5
Mews La SO22 3 A3
Middle Brook St SO23 3 D3
Middle Rd SO22 3 A2
Middle Vw SO22 3 A2
Mildmay Ct SO23 3 E3
Mildmay St SO22 10 C1
Mill Hill SO24 16 D3
Mill La SO21 7 H4
Milland Rd SO23 9 F6
Millers Yd SO21 5 B2
Milman Ct SO23 3 D2
Milner Pl SO22 8 D6
Milnthorpe La SO22 3 A4
Milverton Rd SO22 8 C4
Minden Way SO22 10 B1
Minstead Cl SO22 6 B6
Minster La SO23 3 C3
Mint Yd SO23 3 D3
Mitford Rd SO24 16 B5
Momford Rd SO22 10 A3
Monarch Way SO22 8 A6
Monarchs Way SO21 13 H2
Monks Rd SO23 9 E3
Monmouth Sq SO22 8 A6
Montgomery Cl SO22 10 C1
Moorcroft Cl SO21 5 C2
Moorside SO23 3 E2
Moorside Rd SO23 9 G2
Morestead Rd SO21 11 H2
Mornington Dr SO22 8 A2
Mortimer Cl SO23 7 G4
Moss Rd SO23 9 G4
Mottisfont Cl SO23 3 C2
Mount Cl SO22 8 C1
Mount Pleasant SO23 7 G4
Mount View Rd SO22 10 B2
Mountbatten Pl SO23 8 D1
Mountbatten Pl SO23 7 G2

Nations Hill SO23 7 G3
Nelson Rd SO23 9 G5
New Alresford By-Pass SO24 16 A6
New Cotts SO21 5 B2
New Farm Rd SO24 16 B5
Newburgh St SO23 3 B2
Newton Rd SO21 13 G1
Nicholson Pl SO24 16 B5
Nickel Cl SO23 9 G3
Nightingale Cl SO22 8 A6
Norlands Dr SO21 12 B4
Norman Flats SO23 9 E6
Norman Rd SO23 9 E6
Norris Gdns SO21 4 C3
North Dr SO22 6 A5
North Hill Cl SO22 9 E2
North Rd SO23 7 G1
North Vw SO22 3 A2
North Walls SO23 3 D2
Northbrook Av SO23 9 G5
Northbrook Cl SO23 9 G5
Northbrook Rd SO23 9 G5
Northfields SO21 13 G1
Northgate Ho SO23 3 C2
Northington Rd SO21 15 F1
Northlands Dr SO23 9 E2
Nuns Rd SO23 9 F3
Nuns Walk SO23 9 F2
Nursery Gdns SO22 8 C4
Nursery Rd SO24 16 D4
Nurses Path SO23 13 F3

Oak Hill SO24 16 D5
Oaklands SO21 4 B4
Oaklands Rd SO23 8 A6
Oakwood Av SO21 12 C5

Oakwood Cl SO21 12 C
Octavia Hill SO22 8 C
Oglander Rd SO23 9 F
Old Gdns SO22 9 E
Old Hillside Rd SO22 8 E
Old Kennels Cl SO22 10 A
Old Kennels La SO22 10 A
Old Parsonage Ct SO21 12 E
Old Rectory Gdns SO21 7 H
Old Rectory La SO21 13 F
Old Station App SO23 15 F
Old Station La SO21 15 F
Olivers Battery Cres SO22 10 E
Olivers Battery Gdns SO22 10 E
Olivers Battery Rd North SO22 10 E
Olivers Battery Rd South SO22 10 A
Orchard Cl, Alresford SO24 16 D
Orchard Cl, Winchester SO23 4 E
Orchard Rd SO21 4 E
Orchard Walk SO23 8 E
Orient Dr SO22 8 E
Otterbourne Hill SO21 12 E
Otterbourne House Gdns SO21 12 E
Otterbourne Rd SO21 12 C
Owens Rd SO22 8 E
Ox Dro SO21 5 E
Oxdrove Way SO23 16 A
Oxford Rd SO21 5 E

Paddock Cl SO21 4 D
Paddock Way SO24 16 C
Painters Fld SO23 11 E
Palm Hall Cl SO23 9 G
Palmerston Ct SO23 11 E
Parchment St SO23 3 E
Park Av SO23 3 E
Park Cl SO23 9 E
Park Ct SO23 9 E
Park La, Abbots Worthy SO21 7 H
Park La, Twyford SO21 13 F
Park Mt SO22 16 C
Park Rd SO22 8 C
Park Vw SO21 12 D
Parkside Gdns SO22 8 E
Parliament Pl SO23 10 E
Partridge Down SO22 10 E
Paternoster Row SO23 3 E
Paulet Pl SO22 10 D
Peacock Pl SO23 9 H
Pearson La SO21 12 D
Pembroke Rd SO23 6 E
Pemerton Rd SO22 8 C
Peninsula Rd SO22 3 A
Peninsula Sq SO23 3 E
Penton Pl SO23 9 G
Penton Rd SO21 13 F
Perins Cl SO24 16 D
Petersfield Rd SO23 3 F
Pigeonhouse Fld SO21 5 A
Pilgrims Gate SO22 3 A
Pine Cl, South Wonston SO21 4 D
Pine Cl, Winchester SO22 10 A
Pitter Cl SO22 6 A
Place La SO23 10 D
Plough Way SO22 10 C
Plovers Down SO22 10 A
Poets Way SO22 8 C
Poles La SO21 12 A
Portal Rd SO23 9 F
Pound Hill SO24 16 C
Pound Rd SO23 7 G

| | | | |
|---|---|---|---|
| ...ces Bldgs SO23 | 3 E2 | St Mathews Rd SO22 | 8 C2 |
| ...ces PI SO22 | 11 E1 | St Michaels Gdns SO23 | 3 C4 |
| ...cess Ct SO23 | 3 D2 | St Michaels Pas SO23 | 9 E6 |
| ...nstead Cl SO23 | 9 F6 | St Michaels Rd SO23 | 3 C4 |
| ...aters Row SO23 | 3 C2 | St Nicholas Rise SO23 | 7 G3 |
| ...ors Barton SO23 | 11 E1 | St Pauls Hill SO23 | 3 B1 |
| ...ors Dean Rd SO22 | 6 B5 | St Peter St SO23 | 3 D2 |
| ...ors Way SO23 | 10 A3 | St Stephens Rd SO22 | 8 C2 |
| ...ary Gdns SO23 | 3 D2 | St Swithun St SO23 | 3 C4 |
| ...spect Rd SO24 | 16 B6 | St Swithuns Ter SO23 | 3 C4 |
| ...dding La SO23 | 7 G5 | St Swithuns Villas | |
| | | SO23 | 3 C4 |
| ...arry Rd SO23 | 3 F4 | St Thomas Pass SO23 | 3 C3 |
| ...een St SO21 | 13 F2 | St Thomas St SO23 | 3 C4 |
| ...eens Mead SO22 | 8 A6 | Salcot Rd SO23 | 9 E2 |
| ...eens Rd SO22 | 8 C5 | Salisbury Rd SO24 | 16 C5 |
| | | Salters Acres SO22 | 8 A1 |
| ...msay Rd SO23 | 7 G2 | Salters La SO22 | 8 A2 |
| ...nsey Rd SO23 | 10 D1 | Sarum Cl SO22 | 8 B5 |
| ...aelagh Rd SO23 | 8 D6 | Sarum Rd SO22 | 8 A5 |
| ...rs Rd SO23 | 4 A5 | Sarum Vw SO22 | 8 A5 |
| ...gent Cl SO21 | 12 C4 | Sawyer Cl SO22 | 8 A2 |
| ...wlands Dr SO22 | 6 B6 | Saxon Rd SO23 | 9 E3 |
| ...nard Moss Ho | | School La, | |
| ...23 | 3 D2 | Headbourne Worthy | |
| ...hmond Pk SO21 | 12 C4 | SO23 | 7 F5 |
| ...geway SO22 | 10 B1 | School La, | |
| ...glet Way SO23 | 9 H4 | Itchen Abbas SO21 | 15 F2 |
| ...erside Walk SO23 | 3 E4 | School Rd SO21 | 13 F2 |
| ...berts Cl SO23 | 7 G1 | Searles Cl SO24 | 16 D5 |
| ...bertson Rd SO24 | 16 C5 | Searles Hill SO21 | 13 F2 |
| ...ckbourne Rd SO22 | 6 C6 | Segars La SO21 | 13 E3 |
| ...man Rd SO21 | 13 F2 | Selborne Pl SO22 | 8 B6 |
| ...mans Rd SO23 | 9 E6 | Seldon Cl SO22 | 10 B1 |
| ...msey Rd SO22 | 3 A3 | Sermon Rd SO22 | 8 A3 |
| ...oks Down Rd SO22 | 10 C1 | Shawford Rd SO21 | 12 D1 |
| ...e Walk SO24 | 16 B5 | Shelley Cl, | |
| ...sebery Rd SO24 | 16 C5 | Itchen Abbas SO21 | 15 E2 |
| ...sewarne Ct SO23 | 3 C1 | Shelley Cl, | |
| ...undhuts Rise SO23 | 9 G4 | Winchester SO22 | 8 B4 |
| ...van Cl SO21 | 4 D3 | Shepherds Cl SO22 | 10 A2 |
| ...wlings Rd SO22 | 8 B1 | Shepherds Down | |
| ...yal Oak Pass SO23 | 3 C3 | SO24 | 16 C6 |
| ...ydon Cl SO23 | 10 D1 | Shepherds La SO23 | 12 B2 |
| ...field Cl SO22 | 8 B1 | Shepherds Rd SO23 | 9 G4 |
| ...ssell Rd SO23 | 9 F2 | Sherbrooke Cl SO23 | 7 G2 |
| ...sset Cl SO24 | 16 C5 | Sheridan Cl SO22 | 10 C1 |
| | | Sheridan Ho SO23 | 3 C2 |
| ...ddlers Cl SO21 | 5 B2 | Shipley Rd SO21 | 13 F1 |
| ...Annes Cl SO23 | 10 C1 | Silkstead La SO21 | 10 A6 |
| ...Bedes Ct SO23 | 9 F3 | Silver Hill SO23 | 3 E3 |
| ...Catherines Rd SO23 | 9 F6 | Silverwood Cl SO23 | 10 C1 |
| ...Catherines Vw | | Silwood Cl SO22 | 8 C3 |
| ...23 | 11 G1 | Simonds Ct SO23 | 9 F2 |
| ...Clement St SO23 | 3 C3 | Sleepers Hill Gdns | |
| ...Clements Yd SO23 | 3 C3 | SO22 | 8 B6 |
| ...Cross Ct SO23 | 11 E1 | Sleepers Hill Rd SO22 | 8 B5 |
| ...Cross Mede SO23 | 11 E2 | Sleepersdelle Gdns | |
| ...Cross Rd SO23 | 3 C4 | SO22 | 8 C5 |
| ...Faiths Rd SO23 | 11 E1 | Somers Cl SO22 | 10 C1 |
| ...Georges St SO23 | 3 C2 | Somerville Rd SO23 | 7 G1 |
| ...Giles Cl SO23 | 3 F4 | South Cl SO24 | 16 B5 |
| ...Giles Hill SO23 | 3 F3 | South Dr SO22 | 6 A5 |
| ...James La SO22 | 3 A3 | South Rd SO24 | 16 B5 |
| ...James Ter SO22 | 3 B3 | South View Cl SO21 | 5 C2 |
| ...James Villas SO23 | 3 B4 | South View SO22 | 10 B3 |
| ...Johns Rd SO23 | 9 G4 | South Vw SO22 | 3 A2 |
| ...Johns St SO23 | 3 F3 | Southdown Rd SO21 | 12 C2 |
| ...eonards Rd SO23 | 9 G5 | Southgate St SO23 | 3 C4 |
| ...Martins Cl SO23 | 3 F2 | Southgate Villas SO23 | 3 C4 |
| ...Martins La SO23 | 9 F4 | Southview Park Homes | |
| **...Martins Trading Pk** | | SO22 | 10 B3 |
| ...23 | 3 G3 | Southwick Cl SO22 | 6 C6 |
| ...Mary St SO22 | 10 D1 | Spar Lane Ho SO23 | 3 C2 |
| ...Marys Cl SO23 | 7 H5 | Sparkford Cl SO22 | 3 A4 |
| ...Marys Ter SO21 | 13 F2 | Sparkford Rd SO22 | 3 A4 |

| | | | |
|---|---|---|---|
| Sparrowgrove SO21 | 12 C4 | The Square, | |
| Spicer Ct SO22 | 3 B1 | Winchester SO23 | 3 D3 |
| Spitfire End SO23 | 9 H4 | The Valley SO22 | 8 B6 |
| Spring Gdns SO24 | 16 B6 | The Walk SO22 | 3 B3 |
| Spring Way SO24 | 16 B6 | The Woodlands SO23 | 7 G4 |
| Springdale Av SO23 | 7 F3 | Three Minister Ho | |
| Springvale Rd SO23 | 7 F1 | SO23 | 3 C3 |
| Spruce Cl SO23 | 4 D3 | Thurmond Cres SO22 | 8 B6 |
| Stainers La SO21 | 4 B3 | Thurmond Rd SO22 | 8 B6 |
| Stanham Cl SO21 | 4 C6 | Tichborne Down | |
| Stanmore La SO22 | 8 A6 | SO24 | 16 C6 |
| Staple Gdns SO23 | 3 C2 | Tilden Rd SO21 | 12 C3 |
| Staple Ho SO23 | 3 C2 | Tovey Pl SO23 | 7 G2 |
| Station App SO24 | 16 D4 | Tower Ct SO23 | 3 C1 |
| Station Cl SO21 | 15 F2 | Tower Rd SO23 | 3 C2 |
| Station Hill, | | Tower St SO23 | 3 C2 |
| Itchen Abbas SO21 | 15 E2 | Trafalgar Ho SO23 | 3 C3 |
| Station Hill, | | Trafalgar St SO23 | 3 C3 |
| Winchester SO23 | 3 C1 | Travellers End SO22 | 8 A2 |
| Station Rd, | | Treble Cl SO22 | 10 A2 |
| Alresford SO24 | 16 D4 | Trinity Ter SO23 | 3 E2 |
| Station Rd, | | Trussell Cl SO22 | 8 B1 |
| Winchester SO23 | 3 B2 | Trussell Cres SO22 | 8 B1 |
| Station Ter SO21 | 12 D2 | Tudor Way SO23 | 7 G2 |
| Stavedown Rd SO21 | 4 A3 | Turnpike Down SO23 | 9 G4 |
| Step Ter SO22 | 3 A2 | Twyford Rd SO21 | 11 F4 |
| Stockbridge Rd, | | | |
| Sutton Scotney SO21 | 5 A2 | Ullswater Gro SO24 | 16 D5 |
| Stockbridge Rd, | | Union St SO23 | 3 E2 |
| Winchester SO22 | 3 A1 | Uphill Rd SO22 | 6 A4 |
| Stockers Av SO22 | 8 B2 | Uplands Rd SO22 | 8 C1 |
| Stoke Charity Rd SO21 | 5 F4 | Upper Brook St SO23 | 3 D2 |
| Stoke Rd SO23 | 9 F1 | Upper High St SO23 | 3 B2 |
| Stonemasons Ct SO23 | 3 D2 | Upton Grey Cl SO23 | 8 C1 |
| Stoney La SO22 | 8 B2 | | |
| Stratton Rd SO23 | 9 G5 | Vale Rd SO23 | 9 G5 |
| Stuart Cres SO22 | 8 C6 | Vale Way SO23 | 5 F6 |
| Sun Hill Cres SO24 | 16 D6 | Valley Ct SO22 | 8 C6 |
| Sun La SO24 | 16 D6 | Valley Hill SO22 | 6 B5 |
| Sunnydown Rd SO22 | 10 A3 | Valley Rd SO22 | 6 A5 |
| Sussex St SO23 | 3 C2 | Vanguards Hill SO22 | 6 B4 |
| Sutton Gdns SO23 | 3 D2 | Vernham Rd SO22 | 8 C2 |
| Swan La SO23 | 3 C1 | Vian Rd SO22 | 7 H2 |
| Swanmore Cl SO22 | 6 B6 | Victoria Rd SO23 | 3 C1 |
| Swift Cl SO23 | 10 D1 | | |
| Sycamore Dr SO23 | 7 F1 | Wales St SO23 | 3 F2 |
| Symonds St SO23 | 3 C4 | Walnut Gro SO22 | 8 C3 |
| | | Walnut Tree Cl SO21 | 4 B4 |
| Tanner St SO23 | 3 E3 | Walpole Rd SO22 | 10 B1 |
| Taplings Cl SO22 | 8 B1 | Walton Pl SO22 | 10 D1 |
| Taplings Rd SO22 | 8 B1 | Warren Rd SO23 | 9 H4 |
| Teg Down Meads | | Warwick Cl SO23 | 9 E2 |
| SO22 | 8 A2 | Water Cl SO23 | 3 E4 |
| Temple Dr SO23 | 15 F3 | Water La, | |
| Texas Dr SO21 | 10 A5 | Abbots Worthy SO21 | 7 H5 |
| The Avenue, | | Water La, | |
| Alresford SO24 | 16 B5 | Winchester SO23 | 3 F2 |
| The Avenue, | | Watercress Mdw | |
| Winchester SO21 | 13 F2 | SO24 | 16 B6 |
| The Beeches SO21 | 5 B2 | Waterworks Rd SO21 | 12 C4 |
| The Broadway SO23 | 3 E3 | Watley La SO21 | 13 G2 |
| The Brook SO24 | 16 C1 | Wavell Way SO22 | 10 B1 |
| The Conservatory | | Waverley Dr SO21 | 4 D3 |
| SO23 | 3 F3 | Wayfarers Walk SO24 | 16 A3 |
| The Crescent SO23 | 13 F2 | Waynflete Pl SO22 | 8 B6 |
| The Dean SO24 | 16 C3 | Webster Rd SO23 | 8 A3 |
| The Drove SO23 | 13 F3 | Wedmore Cl SO23 | 10 A3 |
| The George Yd SO24 | 16 D4 | Weeke Manor Cl SO22 | 8 B2 |
| The Hall Way SO22 | 6 A5 | Well House La SO22 | 6 C5 |
| The Paddock SO23 | 7 G4 | Welshers La SO21 | 10 C6 |
| The Pastures SO23 | 7 F1 | Wentworth Grange | |
| The Row SO21 | 15 E4 | SO22 | 8 D6 |
| The Soke SO24 | 16 D3 | Wesley Rd SO23 | 7 G2 |
| The Spinney SO21 | 12 C1 | Wessex Dr SO22 | 8 C2 |
| The Square, | | West End Cl SO22 | 3 A2 |
| Sutton Scotney SO21 | 5 B2 | West End Ter SO22 | 3 A2 |

| | |
|---|---|
| West Field Rd SO23 | 7 G1 |
| West Hill Pk SO22 | 8 C4 |
| West Hill Rd North | |
| SO21 | 4 C3 |
| West Hill Rd South | |
| SO21 | 4 D3 |
| West St SO24 | 16 D4 |
| Western Rd SO22 | 3 A1 |
| Westfield Rd SO22 | 6 A5 |
| Westley Cl SO22 | 8 B2 |
| Westman Rd SO22 | 8 B2 |
| Westminster Gate | |
| SO22 | 8 A6 |
| Wharf Hill SO23 | 3 F4 |
| Wheatland Cl SO22 | 10 C1 |
| Wheelers Yd SO21 | 5 B2 |
| White La SO21 | 11 F6 |
| White Swan Ct SO21 | 5 B2 |
| Whiteshute La SO23 | 11 E1 |
| Wilberforce Cl SO22 | 8 B6 |
| Willis Waye SO23 | 7 G4 |
| Winchester By-Pass | |
| SO23 | 9 H1 |
| Winchester Hill SO21 | 5 B3 |
| Winchester Rd, | |
| Alresford SO24 | 16 A6 |
| Winchester Rd, | |
| Compton End SO21 | 10 D6 |
| Winchester Rd, | |
| Otterbourne SO53 | 12 A6 |
| **Winchester Trade Pk** | |
| SO23 | 9 H3 |
| Windermere Gdns | |
| SO24 | 16 D6 |
| Windsor Ho SO23 | 3 E2 |
| Windsor Rd SO24 | 16 B5 |
| Winnall Cl SO23 | 9 G3 |
| **Winnall Ind Est** | |
| SO23 | 9 H2 |
| Winnall Manor Rd | |
| SO23 | 9 G3 |
| Winnall Valley Rd | |
| SO23 | 9 G4 |
| Winslade Rd SO22 | 6 B6 |
| Winton Cl SO22 | 8 D2 |
| Witton Hill SO24 | 16 C5 |
| Wolfe Cl SO23 | 10 B5 |
| Wolvesey Ter SO23 | 3 F4 |
| Wonston Cl SO23 | 5 C2 |
| Wonston La, | |
| South Wonston SO21 | 4 A1 |
| Wonston La, | |
| Sutton Scotney SO21 | 5 C3 |
| Woodfield Dr SO22 | 8 A6 |
| Woodgreen Rd SO23 | 6 B6 |
| Woodland Dro SO21 | 13 F5 |
| Woodlands Ct SO23 | 9 E2 |
| Woodlea Cl SO22 | 8 D1 |
| Woodpeckers Dr SO22 | 8 B2 |
| Woolford Cl SO23 | 8 B6 |
| Woolverston SO22 | 8 C2 |
| Wordsworth Cl SO22 | 8 C3 |
| Worthy Ct SO23 | 7 G4 |
| Worthy La SO23 | 3 C1 |
| Worthy Rd SO23 | 9 E3 |
| Wren Cl SO22 | 10 D1 |
| Wrights Cl SO21 | 4 B3 |
| Wrights Way SO21 | 4 C3 |
| **Wykeham Ind Est** | |
| SO23 | 9 G2 |
| Wykeham Pl SO22 | 8 B6 |

For an up-to-date publication list and latest prices visit our web site at

# www.estate-publications.co.uk

Use the search facility to find the village, town or city you require.

## Local Red Books (selection of)

Ashford & Tenterden
Barnstaple & Bideford
Basildon & Billericay
Basingstoke & Andover
Bath & Bradford-upon-Avon
Bedford
Brentwood
Bromley (London Borough)
Burton-upon-Trent & Swadlincote
Cambridge
Chelmsford, Braintree & Maldon
Chester
Chesterfield
Chichester & Bognor Regis
Colchester & Clacton
Crewe
Eastbourne, Bexhill, Seaford & Newhaven
Exeter & Exmouth
Fareham & Gosport
Folkestone, Dover, Deal & Romney Marsh
Gloucester & Cheltenham
Gravesend & Dartford
Great Yarmouth & Lowestoft
Hereford
Ipswich & Felixstowe
Kidderminster
Kingston-upon-Hull

Lancaster & Morecambe
Lincoln
Macclesfield & Wilmslow
Maidstone
Medway & Gillingham
Newport & Chepstow
Northampton
Norwich
Nuneaton & Bedworth
Oxford & Abingdon
Peterborough
Plymouth, Saltash & Torpoint
Reading & Henley-on-Thames
Redditch & Bromsgrove
Rugby
Salisbury, Amesbury & Wilton
Sevenoaks
Southend-on-Sea
Stafford
Swindon
Telford
Tunbridge Wells & Tonbridge
Warwick & Royal Leamington Spa
Weston-super-Mare & Clevedon
Winchester
Wolverhampton (Sheet Map)
York

## Super Red Books

Birmingham (Colour)
Bournemouth
Brighton
Bristol
Cardiff
Coventry
Derby
Edinburgh
Glasgow
Leicester
Nottingham
Portsmouth
Southampton (Colour)
Stoke-on-Trent
Swansea

## County Red Books

Bedfordshire
Berkshire
Buckinghamshire
Cambridgeshire
Cheshire
Cornwall
Derbyshire
Devon
Dorset
Essex
Gloucestershire
Hampshire
Herefordshire
Kent
Leicestershire & Rutland

Lincolnshire
Norfolk
Northamptonshire
Nottinghamshire
Oxfordshire
Shropshire
Somerset
Staffordshire
Suffolk
Surrey
Sussex (East)
Sussex (West)
Warwickshire
Wiltshire
Worcestershire

Estate Publications, Bridewell House, Tenterden, Kent, TN30 6EP
Tel: 01580 764225   Fax: 01580 763720